A Stirring in the Dark

Christina Lovin

Old Seventy Creek Press
Poetry Series 2012

OLD SEVENTY CREEK PRESS POETRY SERIES 2012

COPYRIGHT 2012 BY Christina E Lovin

2012 OLD SEVENTY CREEK FIRST EDITION

PRINTED IN THE UNITED STATES OF AMERICA
ALL RIGHTS RESERVED UNDER INTERNATIONAL
AND PAN-AMERICAN COPYRIGHT CONVENTIONS
PUBLISHED IN THE UNITED STATES
BY OLD SEVENTY CREEK PRESS

RUDY THOMAS, PUBLISHER
P. O. BOX 204
ALBANY, KENTUCKY 42602

**ISBN-13: 978-0615708218 (Old Seventy Creek Press)
ISBN-10: 0615708218**

Acknowledgements

Poems in this book have appeared in the following journals and anthologies. Some also appeared in *What We Burned for Warmth* & *Little Fires*, Finishing Line Press.

American Poetry Journal: "False Map."
A Quiet Shelter There: "Shadow"
The Bark: "Shadow"
Beloved on Earth: 150 Poems of Grief and Gratitude: "Swedish Rye"
Best Poem: "Photograph, 1975."
Bigger Than They Appear: "The Zen of Mountain Driving"
Caesura: "Late Cicada"
Canary: "Little Fires"
Coal: An Anthology: "Coal Country" (excerpt)
Come Together: Imagine Peace: "This Day in Particular"
Crab Creek Review: "Creature Comforts"
Diner: "In the Garden of Carnivorous Plants"
Entelechy International: "At Grandmother's Funeral," "Erosion,"
Family Photos (Capital Bookfest Anthology): "Reading Tea Leaves"
From the Other World: Poems in Memory of James Wright: "Two"
Georgetown Review: "Clear Cut"
Harvard Summer Review: "North Side of the House"
The Heartland Review: "General Semantics and the Moles on Your Back"
Hunger Mountain: "Deep Shade"
In Our Own Words/People Before Profits: "Overburden"
In the Eye (anthology): "This Day in Particular"
Kentucky Quilt Trail (KAC) "A Small Universe," "Devotion"
Liaisons II: "Two," "False Map," "Snapping Turtle," "Overburden"
Light in Ordinary Things: "Bucket Man," "A Small Universe," "Creature Comforts"
Love After 70: "Photograph, 1975"
Love Over 60:100 Women Poets Over 60: "Two"
Mid-America Poetry Review: "Snapping Turtle"
Missing Mountains: We went to the mountaintop but it wasn't there: "Overburden"
New Millennium Writing: "Never Tell"
New Southerner Anthology: "The Zen of Mountain Driving" "Homing"
Northern New England Review: "circa 1795"
Off the Coast: "Eating the Purple"
Once a Garden: "In the Garden of Carnivorous Plants"
Passager: "Coal Country"
Poemeleon: "At Dripping Spring"
Poesia: "Coal Country"
Presence: "A Small Universe"
Prism Quarterly: "Inheritance"
Public Republic: "Two"
Sailing in the Mists of Time (anthology): "Coal Country"
Stimulus Respond: "Settlement," "North Side of the House," "Two" "Shadow"
Susan B & Me: "Inheritance"
Touching: Poems of Love, Longing, and Desire: "General Semantics…"
Trellis Magazine: "Monet's Diary"
Vacations: The Good, the Bad, And the Ugly: "The Stones at Lucia Beach"
Writers' Place Anthology: "A Stirring in the Dark"

In deep gratitude to Kentucky Arts Council, Kentucky Foundation for Women, and the Elizabeth George Foundation; without their support, this book might never have been written; Vermont Studio Center, Virginia Center for the Creative Arts, Prairie Center for the Creative Arts, Spring Creek Project, Friends of Connemara, Devil's Tower Writers and the National Park Service for providing time and space to work on these poems.

Contents:

Green Darkness

Page 7 Shadow
Page 8 Little Fires
Page 10 Overburden
Page 12 Clear Cut
Page 16 False Map
Page 18 Snapping Turtle
Page 19 The Zen of Mountain Driving
Page 20 Homing
Page 21 Late Cicada
Page 22 This Day in Particular
Page 24 A Small Universe
Page 25 At Dripping Spring
Page 27 Bucket Man
Page 28 Creature Comforts
Page 29 Two

Supper in the Dark

Page 31 General Semantics and the Moles on Your Back
Page 32 Erosion
Page 33 Settlement
Page 35 In the Garden of Carnivorous Plants
Page 36 Somnambulation in Blue
Page 37 The Stones at Lucia Beach
Page 38 circa 1795
Page 39 Eating the Purple
Page 40 Clearing the Hill
Page 42 Devotion
Page 43 Monet's Diary: Devil's Tower, Wyoming, 1896
Page 45 Coal Country

The Dark Shapes' Meanings

Page 50 Never Tell
Page 51 At Grandmother's Funeral
Page 52 Deep Shade
Page 53 North Side of the House
Page 54 Inheritance
Page 55 Photograph, 1975
Page 56 Keeper
Page 57 Swedish Rye
Page 58 Reading Tea Leaves
Page 59 Event Horizon
Page 63 Unmarked Crossing
Page 65 Family Plot, Memorial Day
Page 66 A Stirring in the Dark

For Jamie, more than he knows.

Green Darkness

Shadow

I want to write my poems like a dog
lives life: muzzle deep in the rot
of flesh and hair found in a far field:
to wallow joyously in the stench
of death—its hard remains worried
until clean and white—and read the shit piles
of life as if they were the *New York Times*
or gateways to enlightenment. Stupid
in my love—all eyes and tongue and tail—
I would head into the path of fate ears pricked,
uncomplaining when its wheel rolls over me.
Just glad to have had this day, this bit of sun
and shadow, some hint of game on the breeze,
a momentary hand resting on my head,

a name to be called.

Little Fires

I.

There are witnesses. There were plans:
Bats would be eased into cold sleep
deep in the bellies of bombers,
strapped with incendiary explosives
the size and shape of their young,
so as not to alarm, but rather when warmed
and wakened, encourage their swift flights
to safety beneath the eaves of paper houses,
balsa wood shops, and flammable factories.
So when their time was up, the bombs
would set off a holocaust of small blazes
across Japan. That was the plan,
and in the trials a million little fires
burst, flamed, then cooled to carbon.
But Praise the Lord and Pass the Ammunition:
the A-bomb came along to "save more lives."

II.

Sometimes the Lord moves in mysterious ways
his wonders to perform. Sometimes He gives.
Sometimes He takes. Sometimes He leaves
the job to his followers. Let him who is without sin
throw the first hammer blow and drive the first nail
to close over the only opening they know: high above
the stained-glass Jesus with his white lambs and benevolence.
Let him who knows the mind of God climb up
to detonate the poison bombs, drop them inside,
and set the final nail. *Come ye who love the Lord
and let your joy, and let your joy be known*
at the screams of the beasts, damned to asphyxiation
because one was lost but now is found, cold and dead,
in the children's Sunday school room, to demonstrate
like a Bible story flannel board how being where one
should not be brings destruction on all one's kind.

Let the faithful stand and be counted like every sparrow
and each numbered hair on each small brown face
pressed against the screen, then falling, falling out of sight,
layer upon layer—two hundred bats or more—snuffed,
then shoveled out, bagged, and dragged to the incinerator.

Let there be a witness. Let it be me. I was the pastor's good wife,
who was not good, who did not speak up, who did not speak out.
Here, I give testimony to their pleading and clawing,
their helpless young clinging, naked and pink,
to their soft undersides. Thirty years, now, and still I weep.
How is it that a true soldier ever sleeps soundly again
with what was nailed over and boarded up,
what was left inside to die? Blessed be the cursed.
And pitied be the bats: feared because they are not beauty,
hated because they subsist on what we detest, what we don't want
anyway, dispensable because they are legion and strange
and do not sing or show bright colors, but are dark
and seek the deeper darkness for their rounds of necessary mercy.

III.

Ghostly in the headlights' glare, chickweed and foxtail
crowd this moonless lane that digs like half-formed memory
between forgetful hills. A bat, two, drop into sight
then shoot straight up like quicksilver moths
beyond the limits of the beams. Another dives
and flies directly at my windshield, but rises sharply
as ash from a wind-killed ember. Mysterious color
of nothing special, a possum ambles in his graceless,
four-handed way along this familiar curve. He disappears
into cinereal straw at the side of the road, pausing
to glance back just once, his eyes black as accusations.

Overburden
with lines from Milosz

We learn slowly, we humans:
overburdened with lessons
taught, forgotten, taught
again in the forgetting
until the lesson becomes mere memory
of diminishing returns:

it was the forest that was holding things
together, not the rock and soil
that we once thought,
just as skin with its many layers
bears the burden of the body
with its many layers, and without
which the flailed flesh weeps and bleeds,
sinew fails, bones part and lean
to aspects of prayer, part
and fall to groveling, then dust.

Try putting the undone
body, felled and split,
back together:
shove the outside in
and try to give it life as if
those disparate parts belong.

There is a saying or there should be:
*Treat the earth as you would your own
body*, for it is your own body:
nowhere less necessary, nowhere
less precious than the rest:

Tree. Stream. Stone. Steep. Least weed.

This is my body, broken for you:

Tree. Stream. Stone. Steep. Least weed:
*Spring Beauty. Fairy Bells.
Squaw Root. Pennywort.
Vetch. Thistle.
False Rue.*

The migratory water thrush circles over
a plateau of waste gray as ash, as if,
by this, she could find her way home.

There is a saying, or there should be:
...pour millet on graves or poppy seeds
to feed the dead who would come disguised as birds.

Clear Cut

I.

Begin here: the place where the forest ends,
where deep shade opens out to garish sunlight.
Edging the slashed hillside, stands of fir attend
the gash, stark contrast to the clear cut's plight:
debris litters the hillside, and below,
along the road, there lays a tire, burned
and slit: *Goodyear Wrangler* still shows
in raised letters. A few yards away, turned
on end, the broken bottom of a Coors
bottle covers the croft in a cottonwood
sapling. The bottle's jagged neck is gored
by a small bough already grown through: the bond
between wood and glass too fast to let go—
until one breaks they stay together, just so.

II.

Until one breaks they stay together, just so
progress can progress: abundance of woods,
the lust for timber for building: that slow
rot system of "supply and demand" goods.
Cheap resources, too much money, too little
conscience. No thought of the futures to come.
See it here, in this landscape of whittled
forest: old snags like teeth broken at the gums:
useless and painful to see. Bleached bones
of the long departed, those who never
made it across the high passes where snows
felled them in their tracks. New growth—endeavors
the color of old fifties—grow innocent
as bombs of the carnage they represent.

III.

Like bombs of the carnage they represent,
the Scotch Broom scrubs explode up this ridge.
Left unchecked, these foreigners will ascend
the hill, then proclaim themselves the scruffy kings
of the dead fern, the felled fir, the skid trail
that scours a swath across the desolation.
Lopped limbs and knots, useless in the board mill,
scatter the site like body parts from a decimating
war between man and forest. We all know
who wins, don't we? Sometimes, the human side
loses a man or two but the *quid pro quo*,
generally speaking, is a rising tide
for the green team: frozen in position,
unable to avoid the demolition.

IV.

Unable to avoid the demolition,
thick-waisted snags from fifty years ago,
rise chest-high the breadth of the hill. Undone
by cross saw when Eisenhower's grow-
ing country needed wood, and interstates
were being planned to snake across the land.
Back when I was just a child these Cascades
were buzzing with removal of such stands
of ancient Douglas Fir. The newest cuts
lie nearer to the ground—their cores still damp,
their stumps still drawing water from their roots
in futile draughts. Lamenting, my boots stamp
depressions in the gravel of the road.
It's that quiet, except for the traffic below.

V.

It's that quiet and when the traffic below
on 126 hums as softly as wind
through the missing firs, spring tree frogs bellow
their insistent chorus around the bend
in the gravel road. A varied thrush sings
its throaty tremolo up on the hill
where oaks stand watch with firs and pines.
There is life here, is there not? Yet we will
grieve the loss of old growth forests—druid
yew, the giant Douglas fir, fragrant spruce—
that lived in harmony with microscopic
beings between the earth and sky. Centuries
of coexistence unlearned, unfathomed.
But look! Ahead I see a burst of red!

VI.

Ah look: ahead, I saw a burst of red
against a six-foot snag: what surely promised
to be some exotic blossom against the dead
flesh of the wood is nothing more than emptied
shotgun shells, shoved down on broken shards
of scar. Man's joke with the forest. But there's more:
in the end we know who has the last laugh. Yards
return to waving fields when left ignored.
You can drive out nature with a pitchfork,
but it always comes roaring back, someone's said.
You'll find it's nothing but a grassy sward
when you leave a road alone with vines and weeds.
Even in this desolation there is hope. Look!
Here on this stump, a stand of moss has taken root.

VII.

Here on this stump a stand of moss has taken root,
and tendrils fine as silky thread raise leaves
like emerald mustard seeds. The gaping wounds
of these old snags swallow water and speed
decay. They nurse new seedlings and promise
to provide a home for fungus and bugs.
Along the trunk, the holes and crevices
show that woodpeckers love these lopped-off logs.
Even the broken bottom of the beer
bottle holds life. I lift it off: brilliant
beetles—tiny jade scarabs—and spiders stir.
Bending closer to the soil, I see resilient
green. Hope, my friends. Some future woodland intends
to begin here: this place where the forest ends

False Map

Double yellow lines center this gray sweep
of asphalt yearning a curve that cuts down
toward the Dix—now a lake—dammed
miles upstream, slow-moving, still
a river at its narrow heart, a sluggish pulse
through palisades—water coming and coming
and coming down from knobs and hills
high fields, sad, rocky valleys, to trudge
imperceptibly between the canyon walls,

and something in me drums—*pay attention—*
look there to the narrow shoulder
of flesh torn—possum, skunk, tuft
of fur, undone gut, exposed claw and tooth
tamed by mortality, remember death
is concrete, and here a something
spans the center lines—rests or dies, lies
motionless it seems as I pass, see it
is a shell still intact, precarious as life itself—

where I've been, where each of us lives
every day of our oblivious lives—twinge,
then pang, then brake, heading back, risk
my own life walking the sharp edge
of pavement with its steep drop to ravine
below where the broken bodies
of empty bottles glitter the black shale
like fool's gold and broken promises,
where a thousand white crosses

for the thousand killed animals are not raised.
Her *whuff* and duck, familiar as my own
unsure reflection in my own mirror: I know you,
little one hidden in your cave of self. Beauty
of yellow-lined leather cheeks, *hiss* and scrabble,
and long-necked log dream: *Graptemys*
pseudogeographica—map turtle. No—false.
Map turtle for the topography of your shell:
fine lines like switchbacks, hairpins, dead men's

curves—*false* for simply not being first.
How you got here, a long mile from river
water, why you came—neither matters.
You don't have to go home, but you know
you can't stay here where a move forward,
a step back are equally fatal, where turning
right or left and following the dual lines,
yellow as cowardice, will get you nowhere
slow. *Come with me. We are both lost.*

Snapping Turtle

I swerved and almost didn't miss her—
dogged in her quest to lay
her eggs in shadowed mire
that lay a lifetime over there,
where pavement ends and earth
takes up again that steady work:
returning dust to dust.

She lumbers on then ducks
and draws herself inside
the carapace whose shades
of brown and gray and black
blend in with shadowed log-soaked
pond but offer no protection
here, where light is hard.

I meet the endless hell-bent cars—
faces disembodied at the steering
wheels speed past—and I recall
a leathered neck and severed head:
it gasped and grasped at sticks
we held before the clouded, open
eyes for half a day, while juicy-hot
flesh fell from the stewing bones
.
I'm past her now, passed over
that thick, meat-filled dome,
five feet from the East side
of the dirt-packed shoulder, fifteen
more to drag across. Northbound,
I wish her a speed not needed
where those branch-thick legs
and graceful webs have danced her
soft in sweet-choked mud.

The Zen of Mountain Driving

Don't brake. Accelerate
through the curves. Press hard
into the steering
wheel with the outside
arm. Relax the inside
grip. Forget the road.
Lean into the arc and eye
the solid line. Unbroken,
let it carry you
around the dark mountain
and safely down.

Homing

The cemetery quiet, no visitors today
save for the somber pigeon holding vigil
on the drive. Some spirit of the dead, earthbound
flight of a lost soul? It came to me, almost,
that bird of common gray and royal purple, banded
on both legs—one in white for courage,
the other black for counted losses. How many
miles from where she started, stunned
and fallen from homing into this tiny square
of ancient gravestones set far from town
in fields of drought-dried corn? Heaven,
perhaps, to a bird—where better to land
than in this quiet realm of death
and food? But now, the pigeon has lifted
to my car window, half-closed. Her eyes
peer at the bird mirrored in the glass; her fear
a mantle she sheds due to her great loneliness.
Even birds desire: that yearning for home
no matter where they land. Even birds,
unknowing of what they know, seek a familiar
roost—if it be a cote or prison.
And I, unwilling to leave her here
where the chestnut is a murder of crows,
where the stippled sky echoes hawk's cry,
where the ground is snake and feral cat,
and every corn row a coyote's trail—
even I, who craved some solitary freedom
on a course that has led me so far afield,
fold her muted wings against her body,
speak softly, and look into her orange eyes,
slip her, scrabbling, then quiet, into an emptied box.
Even I, knowing she may never find her way back
from where she came, knowing safety is a place
sometimes that is nowhere close to home,
drive out down this cobbled, narrow lane lined with strong-
armed maples holding back the fields and the open sky.

Late Cicada
 9/11/2001

September evening opens
like a puzzle box: secrets revealed
and hidden once more
slide in and out like shadows
echoing shadows.

Press your ear to the opening
of the earth: the body
yearns to learn precisely
the tone between the cracks
of cicada shells and the pealing
modulation that follows:

forgetting the silent years
beneath the soil—still and cold
as lost minutes grieving—
where day and hour, past
presence, the transforming
light of seasons had no place,
their singing clings in the present
arms of the crucified pear tree:
strains of just this very night
and only here: this moment
after the fall of fruit
heavy with sweet decay,
even though, even now,
hollow shells grip the ground
like an early frost.

This Day in Particular
    9/11/2002

You mowed the mares' field yesterday
because the sky was clear, the air dry,
and would be so for days to come, or so
the Farmer's Almanac had claimed.

Today, the baler swept the field of loosely
mounded timothy and clover, swirling
up and over, tidying the strewn field,
leaving only stubble. "I haven't cut

the feet from off one rabbit," you say. I hear
the echoes of your mother's hills
in the modulation
of your voice, as you tell me of the time

a sucker snake was caught up, bound
into a bale, dying there, and how the hay,
pressed around the rotting flesh, would have decayed.
So, you spread and fed it fresh to mares and foals

that leaned the fence beside the barn. You tell me
that too many horses spoil a tract of grass:
their droppings soil the hay,
rendering it inedible and sour.

You say there is a man you know who
sheared the legs from off twin fawns.
Hidden in the tall grass, startled to a run,
they skittered from the tractor's wheels, only

to meet the mower blade eight feet
to the side. How he didn't have a gun
but in plain sight of his grandsons, seven
and five, he hammered the deer skulls to death's

mercy. But today, not one rabbit, snake, or fawn.
No small child to witness. Only firm, fresh
bales that wait to be unbound and split
to ease winter-hungry bellies of animals

held stamping in their stalls or snowbound
in the fields. And in that cold
the fragrance of September's grass
will rise like prayer and you will not remember

this day in particular, just the rest that comes
at the end of the sweat, these blameless bales
towering to the haymow's
rafters, the sacred smell of the living

creatures, the blessed soil.

A Small Universe

Darkness full of radiance and resonance:
heavy boots biting the gravel beside me,
sway of your body, or the wind, or your breath—
some air moving somewhere—
and simply the most fireflies I've ever seen:
each side of the lane pasture grasses rise
and raise stars into stars. You turn off
the strong light of safety for me to better see,
while up the way, frogs boom and pipe,
their jewel eyes floating on the dim pond.

Three stallions you will geld tomorrow—
ghosts against the black barn—
whicker to the ridiculous month-old colt
and his sleek, fat mother two fields away.
Across the gap, the neighbor's donkeys
bray to the night, and off what seems too close,
coyotes lift long faces skyward as if their songs
could stop the moon's intrusion.

I close my eyes but still see celestial sparks
that bloom, a small universe,
behind my violet eyelids. Blood rhythm
pounds my ears like any hollow thing drummed,
and I can't help but breathe in this living night:
the promise of fresh manure, last summer's
hay—unbound and spread—sweat from your day's work,
and some sweet stench—indistinct, compelling—
rising from the opened furrows.

At Dripping Spring

Turn right, he says and she obeys, then stops the car
before a swell of creek that writhes beside the road.
Why did you stop? He asks. *This is a road.* He says.
He smiles at her bewilderment. *Turn left now. This is a road.*
And having faith in him and all he seems, she eases down
into the stream, the current running hubcap high,
tires grazing solid stone as wide as any country lane,
then follows it along downstream,
to where the tracks of other wheels rise up the bank
on grass worn down beneath the shade of walnut trees,
and elms tall as her childhood memories,
protected here from storm and ravaging disease.

Engine quiet now, the sound of running water
resonates above the scolding of the crows.
An open mouth of darkness—half-stopped with stone
to press the small cave closed and seal the secret throat—
spills cold, clear water from that fissured cleft,
through a mossy pipe and out from earth
into the overflowing trough. *It never stops.*
He says. E*ven in the driest times*. And she can see
from where the water springs, distilling through the hill
above where fields grow wild with fescue,
where earth is stony loam, down through the soil,
through sand and gravel— forced between the plates
of shale day after summer day, or trickling
thickly from the numbed maw of winter.

He bends to gathering, careful with the shrunken skins
of walnuts blackened on the ground,
knuckling the firm green hulls of the newly fallen
without regard, dropping all into a plastic bag
she finds among the litter left by partiers and lovers.
A buckeye falls. Or just another walnut in its simple casket?
The quiet startles up with the insult of an unseen bird
and peace is shattered for a moment, then reassembles
at their feet. He reaches down, then tucks
a brown -eyed kernel in her palm,
closing both their fingers over that cool, smooth skin.

Water lisps the worn lip of stone in constancy—
around and down into the stream below and out to sea
at some bright point a thousand miles away—
tires slip down the bank into the stream, drag
across the dark flow, up the other side to open road.

Bucket Man
~for James

Drive down any road here
strewn with peeled-off rubber
retreads, ubiquitous

halves of lots of pairs of
shoes, broken boards, hubcaps,
road kill in diverse states

of decay. Useful things,
too—for he slows the truck,
stops beside the pavement,

dodging oncoming cars
to cross the road. Retrieves
the prize from that weedy

muck of ditch—a bucket,
handy for carrying
sweet mash or barley to

horses, water to quench
their mighty thirsts. Buckets
from construction trucks, those

pails that held plaster and
joint compound, nails, or paint,
and shortening vats from bakeries—

washed and dried—are of use
on a farm. If you find one,
hold on to that bucket

man—who better to know
the value of some lost,
some used and empty thing?

Creature Comforts

Because I could not feed the world,
I threw crumbs and peelings to the birds
and gave my little dog the all-but-finished dinner
plate, on which I'd left a cube of meat,
a gravy smear.

Because I could not clothe all children,
I tied scraps of sturdy corduroy to trees
and scattered bits of ribbon on the rising wind
from which the wrens could weave a cozy nest
for naked young.

Because I could not find a home for all
who sleep and weep beneath an arch of bridge
in boxes stuffed with rags and grief,
I piled an extra fork of straw in stalls
and made a bed beneath the stairs for my two cats
to doze and dream.

Because I cannot find a way to hold
the wild-eyed owl, the black-soul timber wolf,
that live untamed beyond the pasture's hill,
that crave the warmth of kill and mate,
I stroke the scar above your brow and love the deeper
those that mark your heart.

Two

> *They love each other.*
> *There is no loneliness like theirs.*
>   James Wright, "A Blessing"

Now there are two. Seven deer, I'm told, before
the cougar's appetite growled: one by one they were taken
down to the forest's soft floor. Just these two escaping:
a tale told by the ragged ear of the one, the nervous
watching by the other. But now they still themselves.
Aware that I am near they do not startle, barely move
across the grass, pause like warm brown statues framed
against trees nearly black in the dusk, but silvery
with mist near their tops. There are two: just enough
to take care of the business of grooming. They stand neck-to-neck,
each licking, nuzzling, teasing the ticks and lice from the other's
coarse fur, enjoying the comfort, the contact, like horses do.
As do humans. As do you; as do I. Touch me here, then,
softly as deer's breath. I will touch you there, where
your mother held you in her arms, your neck against her shoulder.
Not where the raging fire begins, where undergrowth sparks
and catches and we are lost in its blaze. No, here,
where the hushed forest opens and the two quiet bodies
have disappeared into the green darkness within.

Supper in the Dark

General Semantics and the Moles on Your Back

The map is not the territory. The word is not the thing.
We see what we see because we miss all the finer details.
— Alfred Korzybski, Father of General Semantics

You turn away and lie with your back to me—
stippled skin stretched over the frames
of spine and ribs. I read the map of you,
a blind traveler tracing the topography—
plains, knolls, vales of your body—
a universe scrolled out on supple flesh.
Your freckles are constellations of dead stars
swept into the black holes of need and too late
now. Sea-lost and wrecked we are, ships without
a chart sliding off the earth's flat face.

I know your body like the road back home
where the way seems sometimes dappled
with shade from tall elms gone
since my childhood, lost to my vision
yet my stumbling feet remember danger
from roots half-buried, like that phantom limb
of my uncle who cried out and grasped
the pulsing emptiness beneath his knee,
feeling the pain of only what was missing.

The word is not the thing, the map is not
the territory. You are not you. You are not
here. Perhaps you are not at all. But
your fluid spine still flows north
from that lush valley and three dusk-colored points
of sandy flesh— intricate as the pyramids—rise
warm between your shoulder blades—
to their mystery and between I fly and am counted lost.

Erosion

The valley is a mile wide here
    where glacier melt coursed through this plain—

now waters trace a narrow mouth
    and part like lips the yielding earth.

My finger where your rings once clung—
    what must have been to leave such marks?

Settlement

Sometimes it takes years. That hunkering down
of a house on its heels to find solid footing.
Girders twist from the grip of beams,
walls lean away, cracking their plaster facades,
then reconsider and stay where they are.
And sometimes in the night a sob eases
through the long bones until breathing
no longer hurts and settlement comes.

In the basement of our old house on the hill,
the mammoth chimney—tons of brick and mortar—
rested on pine slabs compressed to less than three inches thick
by the weight of two hundred—and five—years:
four fireplaces, their worn hearths, a beehive
oven, two flues, lined against fire—heavy with creosote
and the ash of what we burned for warmth.

I opened your letter today: precise list
of gathered possessions, the meager assets,
    our great debt.

How little it all comes down to in the end:
    shares, bought high, held too long,
    life insurance borrowed heavily against,
    little saved, less in hand:
    paintings picked more for form and color than art's sake,
    that Castillo B we bought on Del Coronado in our first year,
    those little antique bird prints we both loved,
    masks from Mexico: an angel and a merman,
    a hand-thrown pottery plate purchased on our honeymoon—
        it fell off the wall and broke years ago—
            the two jagged halves packed away,
    the washboard from my father's jug band days, emblazoned,
        Maid Rite,
    your grandfather's pipe, bowl burned out, the stem chewed, short,
    Bose and Macintosh you acquired back in '71,
        years before we met,
    a cherry wood bed I brought with me from my first marriage—
        the mattress only you and I shared.
You give up what is no longer precious.
I concede what is not need or sentiment.
The remainder we will sell to strangers.

Someday, I will drive back toward the river.
Halfway down that slow hill, I know
the house will still stand, grounded on granite.
Tall despite its age, it will seem to lean a little
and I'll remember the corner post is rotted,
recall the old slope to the bedroom floor
from the hallway door to the window.
The whole house will have slumped a little more
around the sagging neck of chimney, even though
someone years ago had tried to fill the gaps below it
with shims and stones, as if some small wedge
of wood or shard of flint could shore it up.

In the Garden of Carnivorous Plants

Even in this night they writhe there
as they did in light thrown slant
against disheveled beds: curious
garden of consuming snare,
male and female grown wild:
fiber of fiber, bone of no bone:
rouge-kissed mouths pursed open:
soft lipped pitchers pouring in, not out,
and florid staffs, erect and veined as flesh,
that rise above the spread of flytraps' fringe
and flange to guard those gaping gates
that once one enters none may emerge,
but only deep and deeper delve
into that secret, sweet, and drunken death.

Was it not with joy we entered,
inebriated by the lure of hope
atremble in our chests like wings
of blue-black wasps shuddering with delight
at sight and scent drawn out
from passion's yawning throat?
Our bites and stings grown futile
in the struggle, we slipped down
and down until there was no longer down
or up but only tall green walls of light
in day and in the night the throb and tick
of outworn wings as struggles ceased,
until our liquefied remains had been absorbed,
drawn down into absolving soil,
our bitter carapaces hollowed, dry.

Somnambulation in Blue

Walk the endless beach at sunset,
picking your way through mounds
of rockweed and decimated mussel
shells. Look down. There at your feet—
every key you ever lost
lies tangled up with blue
dental floss and used condoms.

The Dalkon Shield you held
drawn up in your body for one full year
lies curled like a dead spider,
the aquamarine legs folded in supplication.
Arranged neatly with gall stones and milky
wisdom teeth, all the nail clippings of your life
create the outline of a face—the crescents cyanotic—
the mouth a straight line. You see it is a pair
of a pair of mating night crawlers,
rigid in their passion, hard and dry
from the stiff inland breeze.

Far out on the waves two figures
skim the creamy foam, shark fins encircle
them in ever tightening orbits—your ex-husband
is making love to your husband's ex-wife,
the two boats overturned, contents
pitching about them—eggs, oranges,
and boxes of store-shelf macaroni-
and-cheese mix bleeding blue into the surf.

You bend to gather up a limb of driftwood—
it is the severed leg of your dead uncle—cold
in your hands, livid and stiff, the veins
like patterned delft against the pearly skin.
Exposed nerves twitch at your touch.
The toes curl. It too leaves you,
disappearing into the smoky gorse
at the water's edge.

The Stones at Lucia Beach

At Lucia Beach there is a stone
where black as secrets
slime spreads below the level
of the lowest tides.

At Lucia Beach there is a stone
that parts that pathway in the woods
where we passed by without a glance,
except to step around and gaze ahead
to where the bay broke
through the pines.

At Lucia Beach there was a rock
we chose to carry home and place between
the creeping thyme and savory—
smooth and black, and wise
for a rock, encircled with a ring
as thin and white as hope,
which never met but left a gap
as wide as this between us now.

At Lucia Beach there is a stone
where rockweed clings
and strokes its feathered fingers
along the ocean's face; where salt
has grooved the grassy flats
and weeps returning tears
into the sea.

circa 1795

Cobwebs gather in a corner of my kitchen
where walls and ceiling meet in pyramidal space.
They sway gently in the insinuated breathing
that disturbs the hushed air of these aged rooms.
Old houses grow crowded where spirits remain who
cannot find doors open to eternity.
                                              One
walks the wide boards above, her scent redolent of
gillyflowers as she passes through the shadowed
rooms, my restless mind. No sound escapes the cold lips,
yet I hear her clearly. She speaks of quiet joys,
mute grief, in this house, which I may only borrow
for a while, although I call it mine.

                                              Yearning eyes
search the distant mists for returning ships…we wait
together at this eastward window. Bearing the
faults of fires two hundred years gone cold, the clotted
glass distorts the fog-bound harbor below. Leaden
sea and shore sway together in their inconstant
embrace. Forever parting—always coming back.

Eating the Purple

At the rim of the hillside,
the garden quavers
with secret delight, coming
into spring. Loosestrife
shares an untidy bed
with wild lupine: white,
some indelicate shade
of rose, that dense hue
of violet. These purple,
the groundhog has stripped
bare with her teeth.
But only these: eating the purple
rods with their scent
of crushed Concord grape,
dark iris lips, split
ripe plum.

Which flower skin
tastes best—
white, pink, purple
folds bent to the
mouth? I only know
my tongue is blanketed
with young fleece
of early comfrey leaves. Bitter
and sweet. But I crave
the musk of
freshly dug beets.

Clearing the Hill

Stubborn roots!
Pussy willow, wild dogwood,
old rugosa, sweet in their bent age, broken
glass, dented tin, weight, net, dredge,
chains—discarded fishing gear:

Clearing the hill below the house, above
the river of salt and undecided tides,
you, granite among the brambles
and boulders, graniteware rusted through
yet beautiful in form and hue,
salvaged for the porch's pansies.

Lilacs will bloom there once more,
the berries we planted will bear, the ache
of awakening will stretch along the branches
of the apple sapling where we meant to plant
our old dog's ashes, but they remain
boxed in the basement of your childhood
home, where you now live
a thousand miles away, alone.

But the cardinal still calls for his mate
and the field sparrow still sings above
the valley of forget-me-not
moving aimlessly down the hill,
toward the sea lavender spreading the shore,
past the seeded scat of woodchuck,
where she once passed just inches from my foot—
a stuffed stole, elegant and sleek,
the tattered pelts of her unfortunate offspring
scattered about the mouth of the den.

I heard the neighbors there lost their home
of three generations. But you and I,
we generated nothing—no progeny
except those that remain open-armed
in the Maine spring, ice fallen
from their bowed shoulders
watering the ground where we unearthed
the bones of what might have been
a child or just an animal; but
we will never know for sure—
left on the back step,
by morning they had disappeared.

Devotion

He leans into the wind, his collar stiff
with gathered sleet and ice, reassures
the animals crowding barnyard gates. *If*

I love you, what business is that of yours?
Goethe asked. Horses return to the barn,
but cattle will lie down in a downpour,

their backs to the weather. He smells wet yarn
and feels a rash begin to scratch and spread
across his chest where years ago she'd darned

the sweater when he'd torn it once again. She's dead
now many years, his wife. He works the place
alone, eats supper in the dark, and dreads

the cold, the night, the morning. Now, his face
a stone, he slams a fist and frees the frozen gates.

Monet's Diary: Devil's Tower, Wyoming, October 1896

The Tower at first sight: chill night
still clings to the wrinkled ancient face
of stone, carving somber shadows
along the Western cheeks, illuminating
the Eastern aspect like Rouen in morning light:
a cathedral ruin rising from the ravaged remains.

Harsh noon, and unlike Giverny, here remains
no soothing remembrance of forgiving night,
only an obsessive illumination:
a wall of brightness against the stark face
of the solitary stack—*the same light
spread everywhere*—defined only by its own shadows.

Today, a blizzard. Even the midday shadows
were softened by that white shroud. I remain
transfixed by the *instantaiety* of the light here, illuminating
each crystal flake as it fell. But in the night
the snow glows upon the brow of that time-worn face:
a deathbed countenance lit by candlelight.

A thaw and yellow leaves of aspens light
up the valley once more, casting away shadows
like earthbound sunshine. As I face
my canvas, I am reminded of what aspect remains
of my subject (and my own life) before night
extinguishes the Belle Forche's illuminating.

Dying day's flame blazes, illuminating
endless sky, holding stone with hands of light
like a man would touch his dying lover's cheek. Night
casts their poignant parting with mourning shadows
and sunset's wash. Chiaroscuro of death against life's remains—
dust to glorious dust—painted on her honest face.

In the darkness, I saw the tower's true face
against the sable sky: A million stars illuminating
the darkest drape, where the North Star remains
as beacon to the lost. But no brush can paint light
where none exists, where only shadows
outline that stack of stone rising black into the night.

And in that night, *what suddenly became clear to me*
    was the unsuspected power of the palette, illuminating
that inanimate mass like Camille's lost and long-loved face,
    showing the soul within. Light,
yes. But shadows, too: haystacks and poplars rot. Rouen will one
    day fall. Camille is gone. *This,* only *this* remains.

Coal Country

I.

What I can't remember and what I can:
my mother washing coal dust from the necks
of Mason jars filled with last summer's jams
and vegetables, their lids and rings black
with grit, contents obscured then visible
beneath the touch of a damp flannel rag
she wiped across hand-printed labels
then dipped again into an enamel pan
where gray water settled from suds to silt.
Those cloths were always discarded, never
used for dishes again, deemed unfit
for the kitchen. Fifty years are over
now: I've known sullied cloth and family:
how some stains never wash out completely.

II.

Some stains never wash out completely
but my mother's mother, Mary, would scrub
worn *camisas* for the soiled but neatly
oiled and pompadoured Mexican railroad-
tie men who came to coal country laying
the wooden ties two thousand to the mile.
Boiled in lye, bleach in the wash and bluing
in the rinse, the shirts emerged starkly white
and innocent as angels. But these iron horsemen
of the Apocalypse, bearing spikes and crosses
for coal and cattle, carried pestilence
with them in that Spring of early losses—
my grandfather dead of flu in '17—
not knowing the damage that would be done.

III.

Not knowing the damage that could be done
we swam in the bright green lake of caustic
water. We thought it daring fun to plunge
beneath the foamy surface, opalescent
with chemicals that oozed unseen from dull
slag heaps: gray hillocks of thick detritus
left from the processing of newly-mined coal.
Knox County was blessed with bituminous
veins, cursed with the scars of its retrieval.
By the sixties, production had slowed down
to a handful of mines that were viable:
the older underground shafts abandoned,
while strip mining left the once-lush landscape stark,
rusted hoppers spilled coal beside old tracks.

IV.

Railroad hoppers spilled coal beside new tracks
as my mother, at ten, scurried along
the crisply graveled rail bed packing sacks
of burlap with the fuel that had fallen
from overfilled cars. On her lucky days
the bags grew heavy quickly and no snow
fell across the hills or, ankle-deep, lay
filling up the trackside ditches below
where the tiny tank town of Appleton,
Illinois, lay crammed into the valley.
And sometimes when the weak winter sun
grew thin as gruel from a caboose galley
kind wind-burned men climbed atop the coal cars
and the black heat was gently handed down to her.

V.

This was how the black heat was handled: First,
the topsoil was peeled back by bulldozers
and piled aside for reclamation. Burst
through with draglines the veins lying closer
to the surface were fractured, making it
easy to scoop the coal from the ground.
Crushed and separated, refined for what-
ever use it was destined: fine powder
for the power plant at Havana, *coke*
for steel, stoker coal for industry, *egg* and *lump*
for the furnaces of homes. Shale, sandstone,
pyrite—*impurities*—were hauled away and dumped
like wasted lives: what helps and what hinders
and what remains: dead ash and cold cinders.

VI.

What remained: dead ash and cold cinders
carried in an old coal hod to the driveway,
dumped in the low places. Rusty clinkers
of stony matter fused together by
the great heat of what warmed our little home
on sharp winter mornings. And in summer
the sunlight spiked off the marcasite nodes:
jewels that scraped and stung, lodging under
the skin of my shins and knees when I fell
from my bike to the cinders and gravel.
White scars remain to remind and foretell:
the last delivery truck of T.O. Miles;
shadows filling empty corners of the coal
room: one small, high window like a square halo.

VII.

One small, high window with a square halo
of light around the ill-fitting metal door:
coal lumps heaped up the walls. Dust billowed
through the air, covering the worn brick floor,
my father's tools stored inside for the winter,
and the many shelves of canning jars, contours
soft beneath a veil of dull black. Heat sent
rising through the grates above and the roar
of the ancient furnace were a living
pulse to which we pressed our ears and bodies
until the natural gas lines reached us, ending
our affair with coal. But like lost love's memories
swept clean, damp days a dark stench still rises and chokes
with what I can remember and what I won't.

The Dark Shapes' Meanings

Never Tell
> *What's past is nothing and remembering
> is not seeing.*—Fernando Pessoa, as Alberto Ceiro

Never tell what might have been—
dull stories of almost but not quite
and never was and who cares anyway
but fools babbling on of the heart
attack survived, the rabid dog outrun,
that turn at the last second—accident
that almost was, but was not—love
un-snared, so how can it be lost?

Move your hand across the bruised
limbs and knotted branches of grafted
apple trees, thick with spring and mourning
of the homeless swarm. Listen
to the high keening of the wind,
of widows—their voices sound the same
in winter—and learn that fruitless melody.
Taste the sea and someone else's tears
to understand your own are bland,
indistinct. New grass forgets
the sharp teeth of frost. Last summer
owns no light; it has been spent
among the high branches of the pines.

Crickets' cadenced dirges, whirring
downward of maple seeds to their own
burial, death rattles in the narrow throat
of the desiccated gourd: herein
lay a hundred million secrets,
but only one revelation, one
certainty—no matter what
might have been, what was.

Remember the trap you set as a child
just to see what could be caught—
crushed wing and broken leg
of the sparrow there, pale flesh
around the surprised round eyes—
how the sun shone down on you
both and on the winter lawn.

At Grandmother's Funeral

She was ancient and demented:
    hallucinating fire and snakes.

At four years, I did not fear her—
    her long gray hair, her yellow nails.

I'd never seen the placid dead.
    I hid from her dreadful beauty.

Deep Shade

Here, once more, my mother at the worn back screen
door, painted white I remember from pictures, in 1939.
That thick stump is again a young maple, green

for mid-October. It's a late fall for Illinois—trees
just beginning to force their sanguinary wines
and my mother, standing at the torn back screen

door, holds a toddler on her hip. He's not yet weaned,
my brother Kent, at twelve months. Philip is nearly seven,
small and wiry as a maple sapling. Gene

is oldest, four years older than Mary. He's thirteen,
she's nine. Merrill, not quite eight, spoke of heaven
only a few days ago. And now my mother sags against the screen—

Poor Merrill's head done bust wide open—a lean,
breathless boy has run a mile to tell what sirens
of approaching ambulances scream as truth: this grief

that will be handed down to me like blood. In ten
years I will be born. It will be October 1949
and my mother will hold me on worn steps below the back screen
door where, in deep shade, the new green paint will seem almost black.

North Side of the House

Moss clings to the dripping tap and rots
insinuate themselves along the sill;
the cellar window slumps
to pulp and fiber, the glass's eyes gone
cloudy with the past. In shadow that refuses
to concede to light, wildflowers rise
each spring to greet the homing geese
as my mother did some forty years
before, when halfway through her day,
she must have known
this wildness I feel now, as she knelt, bent
spoon in hand, the forest seeping
dampness, cold against her roughened knees,
to scoop reclusive seedlings
and carry them in mopping pails
to the north side of the house:

Dutchman's pants, in innocence as white as first tooth
lost and saved, wave on their slender lines like flags
at Swellendam and Graaf Reinet.

Jack, the fundamental preacher, wags his disapproving head
beneath the flourished sounding-hood, his pulpit
high upon its safe and solitary stalk.

Spring Beauty lifts her vacant lovely face
with starry gaze and thin-lipped smile
accepting this, her banished fate, with grace.

Separation sighs through Trillium leaves,
pulsing purple blooms like that which flames
behind clenched lids.

The secret pain of Blood Root pushes
deep beneath the dirt, bleeding
fingers reach for what they cannot hold.

Like them, I bloom in shade
where I do not belong—sad soil
clings to my roots like bits of cradlesong
stick in the ear across the silenced
years, and sings with tears that choke
me back to where the nettles
bite and sting.

Inheritance

I eat the food my mother cooks and serves.
At ninety-three, she waits on me and death
with equal patience and expenditure
of energy, measuring out the breadth
and height of every breath. Her days slice thin
as apples for the pies she knows by heart:
the spices stale within the dusty tins,
that pinch of salt that livens flour and lard,
shrunken fruit as wizened as her face,
the circle that she rolls without a tear
and smooths into her mother's granite plate.
Her table like her life now, is small and square.

Her shuddering blade divides the weeping pie—
the lacerated pastry seeps and sighs.

Photograph, 1975

My mother in a red coat, reclining
in the prow of a gray row boat. Gray all around.
Gray the sky. Gray the water. Gray her eyes,
although my father always called them blue.
This, in their fiftieth year together—
the children grown and gone—my father unseen
behind the camera. My mother's look coquettish
and young as any lover in this autumn shot.

Thirty years later, ten years past his death—
her health gone, four of seven children gone, gone
that bloom about her which even I, the youngest,
remember—she wastes in bed to skin and broken bone.
Your father was a keeper, she states one day
for no apparent reason. Him being only Father to me
I fail to understand. Until, when going through her things,
I pull this photo, whole, from a box of ruined prints.

Keeper
*You have to be smarter than
the fish.* Bob Ericson, 1908-1995

My father's heart was an old boat—
wrecked and mended,
the knots tied all wrong for a sailor at sea
but safe enough it seemed
for us to loose the moorings
and row the lake of him.

He became the drop and pull,
the lift of our oars: troubled
water and suspended motion
over the bright lagoon of childhood—
ripples stirred and yearning
toward a shore never reached.

His big dreams were little minnows
taken, one by one,
threaded on hooks and worried
by large-mouthed bass and saw-toothed pike
that lurked in murky places
where disappointment clung like wrack
to our sunken family tree.

Anchor set, he was.
Lure and hook and worn
green filament, weary of use.
Snagged and taut, he snapped
like twenty pounds on 5 lb. test,
the broken ends unraveling:
one falling back empty, frayed,
the other sucked down below
the broken surface—
leader lost, sinker sunk,
keeper that got away—
the old bullhead glimpsed,
whisker and spine,
in the turbid shallows.

Swedish Rye

What is it that I fear to smear like grease
across the starched white apron
of this page? Memories that cling and prick
like caraway between the teeth:

my father singing in the kitchen
as he kneaded dark rye dough
across a wooden board,
his hands full of the mystery of yeast
and flour—full of Illinois prairie sun,
tan and firm—working gluten lumps
from the raw bread. Crusted toughly—
the loaves he formed—thick-skinned
and earthy. Hard to chew,
harder to swallow.

Last time I bent to kiss his head
the skin was crisp and brown,
a taste of salt rising on my lips,
taking me home only to leave me
an orphan in the empty kitchen,
the oven open-mouthed and cold.

Reading Tea Leaves

*Drain the fragrant liquid, drink
in the scent of jasmine—*
my mother taught me this—
tip the cup, translucent as time, fragile
on its impossibly thin rim, drops
the color of old blood seeping
onto the saucer beneath:
*three quick turns clockwise
        to set the past*
to approach the future—
her mother taught her this—
        *lift the cup and peer into its open mouth
        to see what it has to say.*

My mother explained to me nothing
of the dark shapes' meanings:
how a lock means obstacles ahead,
how a mask is a secret that must be kept,
how scattered beads of a broken necklace
        show danger ahead in love,
        how an army of ants signals a host
                of impending difficulties.

We sat together on winter evenings,
my mother and I, in a cool ring of light
illuminating Formica and chrome,
imagining brown-stained blossoms as hope,
picturing houses—the signs of comfort—
under trees, which signal health,
our fast friends as dogs, and
stems and sticks that became the figures
of those who would surely come to visit
if we made out their initials nearby.

No time for boiling, stirring, straining—my tea is in bags now:
    every house of comfort washed away
    the dogs long dead and buried.
The lip of cup is mute, escaped flecks choking the open throat
    (gathering ants or scattered beads, what does it matter?)
    dipped and drained, the leaves sulk in silence
    within their shroud of mesh with its tether of string
    wherein all the letters of the alphabet are drawn.

Event Horizon

I.

The laws of physics meant nothing to me—
young girl at my desk, seventeen and full
of what I thought maturity. Already
engaged—ready to be rid of the dull
teacher with his chalk-dusted suit, the loud
ties, and droning voice—thinking of the sex
married women have: no worries about
parents, cops, or gossip. The girl whose desk
was next to mine was pregnant by October,
her disappearance from our class no shock,
just simple math—knocked up by an older
boy: how one plus one makes three. No log-
arithms needed, no cosines: the quantum
consequences expanding from the sum.

II.

Consequences expanding from the sum
of her ninety-seven years, my mother fell:
the blunt force of an object in motion
against an object at rest, the floor. Frail
frame unable to stand up to Newton's
first law in which *a body continues
in velocity unless acted upon
by an external force,* bones and sinew
failed, tortured like laundry in the wringer
washer she used to use. *What a fellowship,
what a joy divine*—I remember her singing—
leaning on the everlasting arms— to the tip
and pitch of an unbalanced load, swells and lulls
comforting her like a bloodless pulse.

III.

Comforting him like a bloodless pulse,
my daughter's car engine silences the baby
riding in the back seat. His sleepy head lolls
to one side as we chatter. It may be
that events are predetermined: the car,
the baby, the two of us. Or are they
random occurrences that execute our
fates: the yearling deer that chooses not to stay
hidden in the roadside brush, but rushes
into the path of an oncoming truck?
Either way, that event horizon pushes
mass and velocity past the realm of luck:
we are safe, the baby sleeps, but the doe,
poor deer, she lies shattered on the ground below.

IV.

Poor dear, she lay shattered on the floor below
her dining room table for hours, waiting
for someone to come. Her footsteps had been slow,
but certain, until then—that day when weighing
a mere seventy pounds (less than half of that
at which I remember her best) the floor rushed
up to blacken all the points where bones and meat-
less flesh collided with the wood. Poor judge-
ment on her part or frailty spun out to its end?
Which came first? The fall? The breaks? Can effects
precede the cause if we are able to suspend
belief in causality principle's next
moves from certain reason to sure result—
the volant object or the catapult?

V.

The volant object is catapulted—
deer by truck—struck heavily, then cart-wheeling—
landing, crushed and broken—life insulted
not by death, but by more excruciating
life--she tries to rise on four fractured legs.
The police are noncommittal on the phone:
Is no one hurt? They ask. I say *The deer,* and beg
for help to end her suffering and mine—
my tears not only for the animal,
but my mother whom I hadn't gone to,
too sick to see her in that last brief fall—
my hospital far from her nursing home—
our separate singularities:
those black holes that merely living guarantees.

VI.

The black holes that merely living guarantees
will suck us in and make us disappear
into the vortex of that mediocrity
principle—where nothing about the deer,
or my mother, or my daughter and her son
is particularly interesting.
Where I am is no more special than
any other place, right? What would Occam
say? Which is the simpler theory—that in which
my mother dying without seeing me was good
or that in which her loneliness at the edge
of death hurled her, cold and unseen as a dead
star into eternity—me, her unlit moon.
struggling with what I couldn't understand then.

VII.

I struggled with what I couldn't understand then
about physics: how if I traveled back
in time and argued with, then killed, my grand-
father, neither mother nor I would be; that
Lambert noticed how *the luminosity*
intensity of light decreases
exponentially with distance as it
travels through absorbing mediums;
and how Lovelock hypothesized that the Earth
is a whole and should be regarded as
a living organism and that each
biological process stabilizes
the environment. But when I was seventeen
the laws of physics meant nothing to me.

Unmarked Crossing

Halfway across is never far enough
at an unmarked crossing when dark gives way

to left and right between rows of tasseled corn
that rustle warning of the coming light—

the last late freight on the CB&Q rushes in
and through to part glass and steel, the living from the dead.

Crush and grind awaken farms a mile around,
but the young girl's ears are stopped with fading sounds of rock

and roll, then static, then the hum of blood. Nothing left
of pulse or nerve when flashlights shine into the wreck.

Who is there to question those who lie
embraced in metal arms, impassive faced—

surprise erased or smashed or sheared away?
Even her father, come to rescue strangers,

could not see the blood that spattered
rail and ties was his—her quiet not of sleep

with gentle stirrings in the restless rooms
of childhood, but this abject silence after the siren's

moan, when crickets cease and startled, drowsing
fowl flushed upward in the night, have fluttered

down to land on the gravel bed, beyond the flame
of flares in lidless eyes that do not see or close again.

And who can answer from the other side?
How else to know she was his own—unmasked

there, blank as a ruined coin?   This is the truth—
for when he later learned it,   he would remember

that the air sobbed, winnowing the grains,
which bent and shook their heads, ears full

of the sounds of not hearing; his own not seeing
and his seeing nothing that had kinship

with the living—that mangled corpse he placed with care
in plastic, drew the closure tight across

the gape, and sent with pity on its way
into the wailing night.

Family Plot, Memorial Day

Redundant stones
face up to the sun:
four brothers and my father
here. I touch each graven
name and leave
behind bending peonies.

Ants flee
the fallen petals.

Robins stalk and draw
long, thin worms
from fresh-turned earth

A Stirring In the Dark

The doctor says it's natural:
vitreous fluid in my aging eye
has shrunk and drawn like old jelly
found in wire-baled Mason jars, cellared
and forgotten. Going pale and breaking
down, the shirred surface has pulled
inward toward the rippled core:
he tells me this is what I see.
But greasy ghosts of jellyfish
keep swimming through my sight
and it appears that empty skins
of snakes have shed their shade
across the brightness of the sun.

For like the moth whose whiteness fades
beyond the limits of the bulb,
a stirring in the dark is all
I catch against the falling light:
the color, or remembrance
of color: my brother's shadow
on the road, stretched out gravel-gray—
he ran behind my bicycle
to hold me up and I could glimpse
our outlines close but distancing
until his stopped and mine sped up
to catch the sun between the spokes.

Or is it someone's half-turned face
reflected in a mirror's fog
just as the steam begins to clear?
I squint to make his features out
but he has turned away and leaves
just emptiness like once I saw
in a wrecked car, whose crazing
windshield shaped and held
the outline of a human head
caving toward the dark inside—
crumbling oval of a missing face.

About the Author

Christina Lovin is the author of *What We Burned for Warmth* and *Little Fires*. Her writing is widely published in literary journals and anthologies. Lovin makes her home in central Kentucky where she collects wool, dust, rejection letters, and unwanted dogs from the Humane Society. She teaches writing at Eastern Kentucky University.

Made in the USA
Middletown, DE
08 March 2017